CW01080691

BOOK ANALYSIS

Written by Cassandra Gibbons

The Woman in Black

BY SUSAN HILL

Bright
≡Summaries.com

SUSAN HILL

ENGLISH WRITER

- **Born in Scarborough in 1942.**
- **Notable works:**
  - *I'm the King of the Castle* (1970), novel
  - *The Magic Apple Tree* (1982), autobiography
  - *The Various Haunts of Men* (2004), crime novel

Susan Hill was born in 1942 in Scarborough, where she lived until her family relocated to Coventry when she was 16. She studied English at King's College London, and published her first novel, *The Enclosure*, while studying. She later described her earliest novels as "very bad... but best to have got them out of the way when young".

A prolific writer, Hill's fiction spans many genres, including horror, crime and children's. In addition to this, she has also written plays, short stories, non-fiction and literary criticism. She won plaudits and prizes for her earlier work, including the Somerset Maugham Award for *I'm the King of the Castle*, and she was shortlisted for the Booker Prize in 1972 for *The Bird of the Night*. She is best known for her 1983 Gothic horror novel *The Woman in Black*, a hugely successful addition to the genre that has sold millions of copies and been adapted into a television film, a stage play and a film.

THE WOMAN IN BLACK

A WORK OF GOTHIC HORROR

- **Genre:** horror novel
- **Reference edition:** Hill, S. (1992) *The Woman in Black*. London: Mandarin Paperbacks.
- **1st edition:** 1983
- **Themes:** ghosts, revenge, death, parenthood, isolation, village society

A classic of 20th-century horror fiction, *The Woman in Black* was published in 1983 and was a huge success. Drawing heavily from the Gothic tradition, it infuses a gloomy, isolated setting with an evil, vengeful antagonist. Set during the early 20th century, the novel follows the story of Arthur Kipps, a lawyer who is haunted by his experiences at Eel Marsh House, where he has been sent to sort through the affairs of a deceased client, Alice Drablow.

The majority of the plot takes place in flashback, with Kipps writing down his memory of events some decades after their occurrence. The use of flashback sees the narrative occasionally interrupted with the musings of the older, present-day Arthur Kipps. The use of first-person narration personalises the horror of the novel, and the tension ebbs and flows throughout.

SUMMARY

THE JOURNEY TO CRYTHIN GIFFORD

Arthur Kipps is a lawyer approaching old age who lives in the countryside with his second wife, Esmé. His life has been marked by trauma, which is why, one Christmas, when his stepchildren turn off the lights in order to tell ghost stories, Kipps cannot handle the spooky atmosphere and leaves. Although he has a ghost story to tell, he cannot bear to talk about it to his family. He resolves instead to write the tale down, in order to try and exorcise the story. Kipps then begins to describe the events of his early career in flashback.

It all begins when Kipps, as a young lawyer, accepts the job of representing the law firm at the funeral of a client, Alice Drablow. He also accepts to sort through her paperwork. He does this because he is ambitious and is glad of the opportunity to prove himself professionally, because he wants to escape the London pea-souper fog and also because he likes trains. He meets a kind local, Samuel Daily, on the train journey to Crythin Gifford, who drives him to his accommodation. Kipps is happy to find the landlord of his accommodation to be welcoming and friendly, but when Kipps mentions that his business is representing Alice Drablow, the landlord becomes cagey and uncomfortable, though he refuses to explain why.

When Kipps is walking to the funeral the next day with a local representative, Mr Jerome, the locals seem to edge away in fright and suspicion, which irritates Kipps. He pities Alice Drablow for having such a sparsely attended funeral, but then notices one more mourner, a woman dressed in old-fashioned black clothes, with a pale, gaunt face. When he leaves the funeral he also notices around 20 children milling around at the edge of the churchyard. When he asks his companion who the woman in black is, he is shocked to find that Mr Jerome almost faints from horror. He reveals nothing, however, and Kipps returns to his accommodation, where he lunches with others who act strangely at the mention of Eel Marsh House, but fail to elaborate. He says: "[...] I was growing impatient of the half-hints and dark mutterings made by grown men at the mention of Mrs Drablow and her property" (p. 57).

THE HAUNTING OF EEL MARSH HOUSE

Kipps waits outside his accommodation for Keckwick, who, with his pony and trap, will take him across the causeway to Eel Marsh House. Kipps is fascinated by the landscape and strangely drawn to the isolation of Alice Drablow's house, even fantasising about potentially living there with his fiancée Stella. Keckwick tells Kipps that he will pick him up a few hours later, and Kipps resolves to relocate temporarily to Eel Marsh House in order to spare Keckwick the bother of coming to and fro, at times dictated by the tide. Before entering the house, Kipps decides to explore the grounds and again spots the woman in black in the graveyard. This time, he is able to view her face more clearly, and though he thinks it impossible, begins to wonder if she might be a ghost. He also senses a malevolence radiating from her being. Upon discovering the amount of paperwork there is to get through, he decides he will return to Crythin Gifford on foot.

When he ventures out onto the causeway, however, he finds it enveloped in a thick fog, and decides to turn back because of the danger that he might wander into the marsh. He hears the sound of a pony and trap, however, and is relieved, believing Keckwick to have returned. It soon becomes apparent that the noise is coming from the marsh itself rather than the pathway, and Kipps is horrified to hear the sounds of a child in distress. Thinking that someone is drowning, Kipps is powerless to try and rescue them without risking his own life. He returns to the house, where he falls asleep, only later to be woken by Keckwick, who has returned for him at two o'clock in the morning, as the sea fret (mist) left him unable to travel across sooner. Kipps realises that the pony trap he heard being sucked under the mud was not Keckwick, and concludes that it must have been a ghostly echo of a tragic past event.

When Kipps asks Mr Jerome for assistance, he again finds him to be evasive and unhelpful. Newly emboldened by his return the village, Kipps decides to return and confront the ghost head on, though he is warned not to do so by Samuel Daily. Daily lends Kipps his dog, Spider, for comfort and companionship in the isolated spot. Kipps returns to Eel Marsh House and begins his work. That night, he is woken with a jolt and realises with horror that Spider is alert at the door, as they have both been disturbed by a mysterious bumping noise. The source of the noise is coming from a locked room and although Kipps tries to get in, he cannot.

The next day, Kipps begins to piece together the story of the woman in black. He discovers that Alice Drablow adopted the illegitimate son of her sister, Jennet Humfrye. That night, the bumping noise recommences, and a frustrated Kipps goes outside to find an axe with which he might break in. Outside he hears the ghostly echo of the drowning child again, and returns to the house to find the locked door open. Petrified, he enters the room and discovers that it is a nursery, and that the bumping noise is coming from a rocking chair that is moving of its own accord. It eventually stops and Kipps leaves the room.

That night, Kipps returns to the nursery in search of a candle, and upon entering, finds himself overwhelmed with feelings of grief and utter despair that are completely unconnected to how he is feeling. When he leaves the room, the feeling leaves as quickly as it came. In the early morning he lets the dog out, only for her to dart out onto the marsh after hearing a whistle. She quickly begins to sink into the mud and Kipps has to summon all his strength to save her. When he returns to the house, he looks up towards the nursery and sees the woman in black staring at him through the window. He again hears the sound of a pony and trap before fainting.

JENNET'S REVENGE

Kipps wakes up inside the house and realises that Samuel Daily has come to Eel Marsh House on a pony and trap and carried him inside. Kipps finally agrees to abandon Eel Marsh House and his assignment and prepares to leave. He takes one last look in the nursery before going. The woman in black is nowhere to be seen but the room has been ransacked.

Daily takes Kipps back to his home, where he treats him with care and helps him figure out the rest of Jennet Humfrye's story. Humfrye was forced to give her son up for adoption, but could not bear to be parted from him and threatened violence until she was granted access. Though she was forbidden from revealing her true identity to the boy, Nathaniel, their close resemblance was apparent, and Nathaniel's relationship with his adopted mother, Alice Drablow, became strained. Before Humfrye could abscond with the boy, as she had planned, he drowned in the marshes while she looked on helplessly from the window.

Jennet died of a wasting disease some time later. Daily also reveals that Keckwick's father was driving the pony trap when Nathaniel died, and that he perished along with him. Daily then goes on to explain that whenever the woman in black has been sighted, a child has died shortly after in mysterious circumstances, including, in one instance, Jerome's child. Overwhelmed with this information, and terrified that another child will fall victim to the woman in black's wrath, Kipps suffers a mental breakdown.

After recovering, Kipps moves back to London and marries Stella. He manages to move on from his traumatic episode and becomes a father to a son. When the child is one, he goes on a pony trap with his mother at a summer fair. While waiting for his family to return to him, Kipps once again sees the woman in black. She frightens the pony, which bolts, and Kipps' son is flung from the trap into a tree, dying on impact. Stella breaks most of her bones in the incident and dies ten months later. Kipps ends his account by coming back to his stepchildren's request that he tell a ghost story: "They asked for my story. I have told it. Enough" (p. 160).

CHARACTER STUDY

ARTHUR KIPPS

Arthur Kipps is a lawyer who lives in the country-side with his second wife. When asked by his stepchildren one Christmas to tell them a ghost story, he decides to write down his haunting experiences with a malevolent spirit known as the woman in black that occurred in his early career. This decision sparks the retelling of the tale, which he writes in the first person.

As a young lawyer, Kipps is headstrong, ambitious and proud. He is delighted to be chosen by his employer, Mr Bentley, to represent the firm at the funeral of Alice Drablow, a recently deceased client, and to go through her papers at her residence of Eel Marsh House. Considering this a semi-promotion, he is content to take on the responsibility, even though it means leaving his beloved fiancée, Stella, behind in London.

Upon arrival in Crythin Gifford, Kipps acts cordially and professionally with all those he meets, clearly buoyed by the responsibility afforded to him by his law firm. He quickly becomes frustrated, however, at the curious reactions when he mentions that he saw a woman dressed all in black at Alice Drablow's funeral. When at Eel Marsh House, he begins to consider the possibility that the woman in black is a ghost, although he is reluctant to truly believe such an illogical explanation.

After several incidents of haunting involving the woman in black, Kipps has no choice but to accept that he is in fact being haunted by her. He handles the situation bravely, deciding not to give up on his task, and even temporarily moving into Eel Marsh House to complete his work. His breaks back in the village always reinvigorate him and convince him to continue; a decision he always comes to regret when he returns and is once again tormented by the woman in black. His resolve ebbs and flows like the tide that traps him at the house for extended periods of time.

When the trauma of the haunting becomes too much, Kipps finally admits defeat and is taken in by Samuel Daily. Before he is able to leave for London, he suffers a mental breakdown, which takes several days to recover from. Nonetheless, from the present day he narrates his recovery and marriage to Stella, as well as the birth of their son. However, he is ultimately unable to escape the wrath of the woman in black, who returns to cause the death of his son and injuries to his wife that claim her life ten months after the incident.

JENNET HUMFRYE/THE WOMAN IN BLACK

The woman in black is the malevolent ghost of Jennet Humfrye, the sister of Alice Drablow who died in her thirties several years after the death of her illegitimate child, Nathaniel. Her story is that of 'the fallen woman', that is to say, a woman living in the Victorian period who had sex outside of marriage and was therefore considered to have 'fallen' from grace. In Humfrye's case, the additional shame of bearing an illegitimate child added to her burden and ostracism from both society and her family.

Forced to let her child be adopted by her married sister, Humfrye was unable to bear being away from her son and threatened violence until she was granted access to him. She was unable to accept that her son was no longer hers, and though she was expressly forbidden from revealing her true identity to Nathaniel, a strong bond developed between the two to the detriment of Alice's relationship with the child. Humfrye was forced to watch from the window as Nathaniel and his nanny drowned in the marshes when their pony trap went off the beaten path. Consumed by her grief, bitterness and desire for revenge, her death some years later was not truly the end of her.

Described by author Susan Hill as an example of pure evil, Humfrye's reincarnation as the ghostly woman in black sees her seek revenge by taking the lives of other children. Any time she has been sighted, a child has died soon after in somewhat mysterious circumstances, be it a supposed accident or unprecedented illness. Humfrye's inability to be happy with her child causes her to seek revenge by denying that pleasure to others, even those who had done nothing to aid the separation of her and Nathaniel.

Humfrye serves as the antagonist of the novel. The horrifying descriptions of her wasted face and ghostly pallor serve to chill the reader, while her inexplicable movements add to the tension of the plot. Her old-fashioned black attire identifies her as belonging to a previous era and conveys her inability (or unwillingness) to move past her grief and let go of her anger and bitterness. Her malevolence, hatred and desire for indiscriminate revenge drive the plot of the novel and are exemplary of the horror genre.

SAMUEL DAILY

Samuel Daily is a wealthy resident of Crythin Gifford who meets Kipps on the train and offers him a lift to his accommodation in his motorcar. He is a very wealthy man, as evidenced by his motorcar (an example of cutting-edge technology of the era), his beautiful house (set in extensive grounds) and his continuous buying of property at the auction.

He is also characterised by his generosity, beginning with his offer of a lift to Kipps. He also invites Kipps for dinner, and, following the events at Eel Marsh House, lets him stay in a spare room until he is well enough to travel back to London, calling in doctors to care for him. He also lets Kipps take his dog, Spider, with him to Eel Marsh

House for company, comfort and protection.

It is Daily who is Kipps' saviour when he faints from exhaustion after rescuing Spider from the marsh. He fills in the gaps in the story surrounding the woman in black for Kipps, telling him that a child has died shortly after each sighting of the woman in black. This allows Kipps (and the reader) to fully understand the wrath of the woman in black. Daily is revealed to be a full believer in the ghost, even though he previously dismissed it as 'women's tales'

ALICE DRABLOW

It is the death of Alice Drablow that triggers the events of the novel. A wealthy, childless widow, her affairs are in the hands of Kipps' law firm. Her existence at the house in the many solitary years leading up to her death was spent in pure isolation, as not only did she live alone, but she also lived out in the marshlands, disconnected from the rest of Crythin Gifford by the whims of the tide.

Drablow is later revealed to have adopted her sister Jennet's illegitimate child, Nathaniel, with her husband. For some time she raised him to believe that she was his mother, but when Humfrye forced her way back into her child's life, it became apparent to Nathaniel (who looked so much like his biological mother) that something was amiss. Drablow's relationship with her son began to deteriorate, and she then lost him to the marshes when he was six years old.

The locals of Crythin Gifford are aware of the details of the story, and seem uncomfortable when Kipps mentions that he is in the area representing his client, Alice Drablow. Her funeral is attended only by Kipps, Mr Jerome and the woman in black. Her house is full of papers that she never threw away and the nursery has been preserved and serves almost as a shrine to Nathaniel's memory.

KECKWICK

Keckwick is a local from Crythin Gifford who has a pony and trap that he uses to transport people (mainly Kipps) across the marshland when the tide is out to Eel Marsh House. He is a man of few words and is abrupt in nature. However, he does come back to Eel Marsh House to collect Kipps at two in the morning (a sea fret stopped him coming at the agreed earlier time) even though it is inconvenient, which shows his good-natured character. When Kipps thanks him, Keckwick tells him that he would not leave him there all night on his own. This suggests to Kipps that Keckwick knows more than he is willing to say.

It is later revealed by Daily that Keckwick's father was the one driving the pony trap that went into the marshes with Nathaniel Drablow. Keckwick's father, like the boy, perished in the incident. Keckwick's quiet nature and unwillingness to talk about the woman in black stems from the loss of his father and his personal connection to the story. The sound of Keckwick's pony and trap creates tension in the novel because the reader, like Kipps, is always unsure if the sound of the pony and trap is coming from Keckwick junior, or is instead the ghostly sound of Keckwick senior's final moments.

ANALYSIS

A GOTHIC SETTING

The Gothic predominates throughout *The Woman in Black*, perhaps most obviously in the novel's setting. The genre typically uses castles, monasteries and manor houses as settings, as these types of buildings lend themselves well to chilling atmospheres, complicated histories and religious backgrounds. Eel Marsh House fits in perfectly with this literary norm with its drab, gaunt appearance and the presence of a small graveyard and the ruins of a religious edifice in the grounds:

> "As I neared the ruins, I could see clearly that they were indeed of some ancient chapel, perhaps monastic in origin, and all broken-down and crumbling, with some of the stones and rubble fallen, probably in recent gales, and lying about in the grass." (p. 63)

The above description implies decay and suggests that the area suffers from extreme weather, which again conforms to the norms of the Gothic; extreme weather can cause lights to go out, can injure or even kill and can prevent people from leaving a building safely. Later on in *The Woman in Black*, Kipps is plunged into darkness in the house due to a storm, and the whistling wind lures the dog into the marshes where she almost drowns. The elements are as much of a danger to the protagonist as the villain of the novel, and the setting is crucial to increasing the sense of danger and dread. And although religion does not play a significant role in the novel, the presence of a ruined monastery adds a spiritual dimension, and is in keeping with the theme of the ghostly.

The desolate isolation of the setting is also an important factor when considering the novel as a piece of Gothic literature. In going to Eel Marsh House, Kipps experiences the total isolation and absence of the (physical) presence of others that Alice Drablow lived with for years. The lack of human companionship adds to the terror of the haunting because Kipps is completely on his own, with no one else to comfort him or protect him. This isolation is broken by the kind and knowing Samuel Daily, who passes Spider on to Kipps because he knows that even the presence of a dog will go some way towards alleviating the fear caused by the woman in black. Although initially drawn to the isolation of the countryside and Eel Marsh House, Kipps soon discovers the way in which solitude exacerbates feelings of terror.

THE VENGEFUL ANTAGONIST

Another trope typical of the Gothic, and of horror in general, is that of the evil antagonist. The existence of pure evil, independent of environmental and external factors, has long been debated, and can surely be debated in the case of the woman in black. Is she an example of pure evil, or does she turn to cruelty in order to avenge the death of her son? Author Susan Hill believes that she is an example of pure evil, and there is plenty of evidence to support this theory. Humfrye's revenge is indiscriminate: she hurts people who had nothing to do with her son being taken away from her, nor her son's death. Kipps, along with his son, Jerome's son and the other dozen or so children who perished played no part in the death of Nathaniel. This lashing out at the innocent implies an innate evil.

The malevolence of the woman in black is reflected in her appearance. The black clothing points to her extended period of mourning and inability to move on from her son's death. Black is also a motif commonly used to represent evil and dark forces, and so in this instance serves a double purpose. Her pale face, due partly to her ghostly state, partly to the wasting disease that struck her before death, emphasises her eyes, from which her malevolence emanates: "[...] her eyes, sunken but unnaturally bright, were burning with the concentration of passionate emotion which was within her and which streamed from her" (p. 63).

Evil is often signified in literature by some kind of physical deformity. The wasting disease that struck Humfrye after the death of her son was a cruel twist of fate: it made people cower away from her even when she was living, and made her even more unapproachable than she was before. It could even be suggested that her hatred and desire for revenge might not have been so intense had she been treated with some kindness after her ordeal. Her unadulterated love for her son suggests that she was, at least at one point, capable of decency. However, the contrasting figures of Mr Jerome, who also lost a child, and Kipps, who goes on to lose a child at the hands of Humfrye, shows that a descent into evil is not inevitable after suffering such a tragedy. On balance, Humfrye does serve as a classic example of an evil, Gothic-style villain.

FORM AND NARRATIVE VOICE

The main events of the novel take place in flashback, told from the perspective of an older Arthur Kipps. The use of the first person is important to note, as the personalised tone used to retell such traumatic events provokes a heightened sense of tension, and inspires more sympathy from the reader than a third person narration perhaps would have done. The testimonial element of the text must not be overlooked either. Kipps himself states in the first chapter that he hopes, in telling his story, to 'exorcise' himself of its power to traumatise him. His use of written testimony, rather than oral testimony (in particular telling his new family his terrifying story), gives him power over the words, a controlled environment in which to produce his story without the unpredictable reactions that he might draw if he were to tell someone. The power of the word is key here in defeating the woman in black, although the reader does not, of course, learn if writing the story down does bring Kipps peace. It is this ambiguous ending regarding any potential closure that allows the novel to continue haunting the reader even after they have finished.

Flashback is used in the novel to simultaneously build and diffuse tension. The first chapter makes it quite plain that Kipps survives his ordeal, which immediately informs the reader that no truly mortal danger is entered into by the protagonist. It could be argued that this detracts from the tension, as the reader knows that Kipps will ultimately be safe. Present-day narrator Kipps also sometimes interrupts the narrative flow of the events he is describing in order to make a remark with the benefit of hindsight:

> "Had I known that my untroubled night of good sleep was to be the last such that I was to enjoy for so many terrifying, racked and weary nights

> to come, perhaps I should not have jumped out of bed with such alacrity, eager to be down and have breakfast, and then to go out and begin the day." (pp. 43-44)

Although this interruption essentially foreshadows the most chilling part of the novel, it manages to increase tension as well, by building up the reader's expectation. The musings of present-day Kipps do not immediately precede the particularly terrifying scenes, and so the reader is tantalised but not completely pre-warned about the haunting at Eel Marsh House. The novel ultimately uses flashback to end on a horrifying note, as the final revenge of the woman in black – the death of Stella and Kipps' son – is revealed. The unexpected horror of the final chapter is shocking because the reader is lead to believe that Kipps overcame his trauma and left the woman in black behind.

FURTHER REFLECTION

SOME QUESTIONS TO THINK ABOUT...

- Can reading a horror novel ever be as scary as watching a horror film? Discuss in relation to *The Woman in Black*.
- Discuss the importance of description and imagery in relation to the setting of the novel. How does this contribute to the novel's tone and atmosphere? Give examples.
- Can you sympathise with the woman in black? Why/why not?
- Discuss the strengths and weaknesses of the use of flashback in the novel.
- Is Kipps foolish or brave to try and continue his work?
- Compare *The Woman in Black* with another work of horror fiction you have read.
- The location of Crythin Gifford is in –shire. Why do you think the author has left the exact location anonymous?
- Discuss the roles played by the secondary characters (Daily, Jerome, Keckwick, etc.).

We want to hear from you!
Leave a comment on your online library
and share your favourite books on social media!

FURTHER READING

REFERENCE EDITION

- Hill, S. (1992) *The Woman in Black*. London: Mandarin Paperbacks.

ADAPTATIONS

- *The Woman in Black*. (1987) [Stage play].
- *The Woman in Black*. (1989) [TV Film]. Herbert Wise. Dir. UK: Granada Television.
- *The Woman in Black*. (2012) [Film]. James Watkins. Dir. UK: Alliance Films, Hammer Films, UK Film Council.

www.brightsummaries.com

Ebook EAN: 9782808016339

Paperback EAN: 9782808016346

Legal Deposit: D/2018/12603/577

Cover: © Primento

Digital conception by Primento, the digital partner of
publishers.